Date Due

Eyewitness Accounts of the American Revolution

Memoir of Indian Wars, and Other Occurrences

Edited by Charles A. Stuart

The New York Times & Arno Press

Reprinted from a copy in
The State Historical Society of Wisconsin Library

*

Reprint Edition 1971 by Arno Press Inc.

*

LC# 75-140883
ISBN 0-405-01211-X

*

Eyewitness Accounts of the American Revolution, Series III
ISBN for complete set: 0-405-01187-3

*

Manufactured in the United States of America

MEMOIR OF INDIAN WARS,

AND OTHER OCCURRENCES;

By the late Colonel Stuart, of Greenbrier.

PRESENTED TO THE

Virginia Historical and Philosophical Society,

By Chas. A. Stuart, of Augusta,

SON OF THE NARRATOR.

MEMOIR, &C.

ABOUT the year 1749, a person who was a citizen of the county of Frederick, and subject to paroxysms of lunacy, when influenced by such fits, usually made excursions into the wilderness, and in his rambles westwardly, fell in on the waters of Greenbrier river. At that time, the country on the western waters were but little known to the English inhabitants of the then colonies of America, being claimed by the French, who had commenced settlements on the Ohio and its waters, west of the Alloghany mountains. The lunatic being surprised to find waters running a different course from any he had before known, returned with the intelligence of his discovery, which did abound with game. This soon excited the enterprise of others. Two men from New England, of the name of Jacob Marlin and Stephen Sewell, took up a residence upon Greenbrier river; but soon disagreeing in sentiment a quarrel occasioned their separation, and Sewell, for the sake of peace, quit their cabin and made his abode in a large hollow tree. In this situation they were found by the late General Andrew Lewis, in the year 1751. Mr. Lewis was appointed agent for a company of grantees, who obtained from the Governor and Council of Virginia, an order for one hundred thousand acres of land lying on the waters of Greenbrier river,—and did, this year, proceed to make surveys to complete the quantity of said granted lands; and finding Marlin and Sewell living in the neighborhood of each other, inquired what could induce them to live separate in a wilderness so distant from the habitations of any other human beings. They informed him that difference of opinion had occasioned their separation, and that they had since enjoyed more tranquillity and a better understanding; for Sewell said, that each morning when they arose and Marlin came out of the great house and he from his hollow tree, they saluted each other, saying—good morning Mr. Marlin, and good morning Mr. Sewell, so that a good understanding then existed between them; but it did not last long, for Sewell removed about forty miles further west, to a creek that still bears his name. There the Indians found him and killed him.

Previous to the year 1755, Mr. Lewis had completed for the grantees, under the order of council, upwards of fifty thousand acres;—and the war then commencing between England and France, nothing further was done in the business until the year 1761, when his majesty issued his proclamation commanding all his subjects within the bounds of the colony of Virginia, who were living, or who had made settlements on the western waters, to remove from them, as the lands were claimed by the Indians, and good policy required that a peaceable understanding should be preserved with them, to prevent hostilities on their part. The order of council was never afterwards carried into effect, or his majesty's consent obtained to confirm it.

At the commencement of the revolution, when the state of Virginia began to assume independence, and held a convention in 1776, some efforts were made to have the order of council established under the new order of things then beginning to take place. But it was not confirmed; and commissioners were appointed, in 1777, to grant certificates to each individual who had made settlements on the western waters, in the state of Virginia, previous to the year 1768 and since, with preference according to the time of improvements, which certificates gave the holder a right to four hundred acres for his settlement claim, and the pre-emption of one thousand more, if so much were found clear of prior claims, and the holder chose to accept it. The following year, 1778, Greenbrier was separated from Botetourt county,—and the county took its name from the river, which was so named by old Colonel John Lewis, father to the late General, and one of the grantees under the order of council, who, in company with his son Andrew, exploring the country in 1751, entangled himself in a bunch of green briers on the river, and declared he would ever after call the river Greenbrier river.

After peace was confirmed between England and France, in the year 1761, the Indians commenced hostilities, in 1763, when all the inhabitants in Greenbrier were totally cut off, by a party of Indians headed by the Cornstalk warrior. The chief settlements were on Muddy creek. These Indians, in number about sixty, introduced themselves into the people's houses under the mask of friendship,— and every civility was offered them by the people, providing them victuals and accommodations for their entertainment, when, on a sudden, they killed the men and made prisoners of the women and children. From thence they passed over into the Levels, where some families were collected at the house of Archibald Clendenin, (where the Hon. Balard Smith now lives.) There were between fifty and one hundred persons, men, women and children. There the Indians were entertained, as at Muddy creek, in the most hospitable manner. Clendenin having just arrived from a hunt, with three fat elks, they were plentifully feasted. In the mean time an old woman, with a sore leg, was showing her distress to an Indian, and inquiring if he could administer to her relief; he said he thought he could—and drawing his tomahawk, instantly killed her and all the men almost, that were in the house. Conrad Yolkom only escaped, by being some distance from the house, when the outcries of the women and children alarmed him. He fled to Jackson's river and alarmed the people, who were unwilling to believe him until the approach of the Indians convinced them. All fled before them; and they pursued on to Carr's creek, in Rockbridge county, where many families were killed and taken by them. At Clendenin's a scene of much cruelty was performed; and a negro woman, who was endeavoring to escape, killed her own child, who was pursuing her crying, lest she might be discovered by its cries. Mrs. Clendenin did not fail to abuse the Indians with terms of reproach, calling them cowards, &c. although the tomahawk was drawn over her head, with threats of instant death, and the scalp of her husband lashed about her jaws. The prisoners were all taken over to Muddy creek, and a party of Indians retained them there till the return of the others from Carr's creek, when the whole were taken off together. On the day they started from the foot of Keeney's Knob, going over the mountain, Mrs. Clendenin gave her infant child to a prisoner woman to carry, as the prisoners were in the centre of the line with the Indians in front and rear, and she escaped into a thicket and concealed herself until they all passed by. The cries of the child soon made the Indians inquire for the mother, who was missing; and one of them said he would soon bring the cow to her calf. Taking the child by the heels he beat its brains out against a tree, and throwing it down in the path, all marched over it, till its guts were all trampled out with the horses. She told me she returned that night, in the dark, to her own house, a distance of more than ten miles, and covered her husband's corpse with rails, which lay in the yard, where he was killed in endeavoring to escape over the fence, with one of his children in his arms; and then she went into a corn-field, where great fear came upon her, and she imagined she saw a man standing by her, within a few steps.

The Indians continued the war till 1764, and with much depredation on the frontier inhabitants, making incursions as far as within a few miles of Staunton. An end, however, was put to the war in the fall of that year, by the march of an army under the command of Colonel Bouquet, a British officer, who assembled, with his regular troops, at Fort Pitt, some companies of militia from Augusta county and other places,—which, I believe, either volunteered their services or were such as were ordered on the frontiers to protect the inhabitants during the war. Colonel Bouquet held a treaty with the Indians somewhere near Muskingum, and the Indians delivered up many prisoners, who returned to their friends, and a peace was concluded, which continued until the year 1774. I do not remember of hearing it alleged by any one, what occasioned the war of 1763, being then very young; but about that time the British government had passed an act to tax the American colonies; but on the remonstrance of the people and the opposition of some of the British politicians, they repealed the law. I have since thought that they were urged to it by private British agency, as it is well known that they were influenced that way to commence the war in 1774. In the spring of that year, General Lewis represented the county of Botetourt in the Assembly, and his brother, Colonel Charles Lewis, represented the county of Augusta, at Williamsburg, then the capital of our government. During the sitting of the Assembly, in the month of April, or May, government received intelligence of the hostile appearance of the Indians, who had fallen upon the traders in the nation and put them all to death, and were making other arrangements for war.

General Lewis and his brother Charles sent an express immediately to the frontier settlements of their respective counties, requesting them to put themselves in a posture of defence. They had, each of them, the command of the militia in their counties, at that time; and I was ordered by General Lewis, to send out some scouts to watch the warrior path beyond the settlements lately made in Greenbrier, which had recommenced in 1769. We were few in number, and in no condition to oppose an attack from any considerable force. But succor was promised us as soon as they could arrive from the Assembly; and, in the mean time, arrangements were made for carrying on an expedition against the Shawanese, between the Earl of Dunmore, who was the Governor of Virginia, and the Lewises, before they left Williamsburg: the Governor to have the command of a northern division of an army of volunteer militia,—or otherwise drafts to be collected from the counties of Frederick, Shenandoah, and the settlements towards Fort Pitt; General Lewis to have the command of a southern division of like troops, collected from the counties of Augusta, Botetourt, and the adjacent counties below the Blue ridge. Colonel Charles Lewis was to command the Augusta troops, and Colonel William Fleming the Botetourt troops, under General Lewis. The Governor was to take his route by the way of Pittsburg, and General Lewis down the Kenawha—the whole army to assemble at the mouth of the Great Kenawha, on the Ohio river. General Lewis's army assembled in Greenbrier, at Camp Union, (now Lewisburg) about the 4th September, 1774, amounting in all, to about eleven hundred men, and proceeded from thence on their march, on the 11th day of said month. The captains commanding the Augusta volunteers, were Captain George Mathews, Captain Alexander M'Clenachan, Captain John Dickenson, Captain John Lewis, Captain Benjamin Harrison, Captain William Naul, Captain Joseph Haynes, and Captain Samuel Wilson. Those commanding the Botetourt companies, were Captain Matthew Arbuckle, Captain John Murray, Captain John Lewis, Captain James Robertson, Captain Robert M'Clenachan, Captain James Ward, and Captain John Stuart.

In the course of the summer, and not long after we received notice of the hostile appearance of the Indians, they came up the Kenawha, and killed Walter Kelly. Kelly had begun a settlement about twelve miles below the Great Falls. When they made the attack, Colonel John Fields, of Culpeper county, was at Kelly's, about to make some surveys on military claims, or otherwise. He had with him, several of his neighbors and one or two negroes. I had sent an express to them, with advice to remove immediately, as it was apprehended that the Indians were about to break out, and I expected they were in great danger. Kelly was, I believe, a fugitive from the back parts of South Carolina, of a bold and intrepid disposition, received my intelligence with caution, and sent off his family and stock for Greenbrier, with his brother, a young man of equally suspicious character. But Fields, trusting more to his own consequence and better knowledge of public facts, endeavored to persuade Kelby there was no danger, as nothing of the kind had been before heard of, and our Greenbrier intelligence not worth noticing. On the evening of the same day, and before Kelly's brother and the family had got out of hearing of the guns, the Indians came upon Kelly and Fields where they were taking leather from a tan trough, at a small distance from their cabin, fired on them, and killed Kelly upon the spot. Fields ran into the cabin, where their guns were, all unloaded. He picked up one, and recollecting it was not charged, ran out of the house into a corn-field within a few steps of the door, and left his negro girl and Scotch boy crying at the door. The boy was killed, and the girl carried off. Fields made his escape, but never saw an Indian. Kelly's brother informed me that he heard guns fire shortly after he had started with the family, and expected his brother and Colonel Fields were killed. I prepared to go and see what was the consequence; raised about ten or fifteen men, and proceeded on our way to Kenawha about ten miles, when I met Colonel Fields naked, all but his shirt. His limbs were grievously lacerated with briers and brush, his body worn down with fatigue and cold, having run in that condition from the Kenawha, upwards of eighty miles, through the woods. He was then, I guess, upwards of fifty years old, of a hardy, strong constitution. He was afterwards killed in the battle of the 10th of October following. A fatality pursued the family of Kelly; for the Indians came to Greenbrier, on Muddy creek, and killed young Kelly and took his niece prisoner, about three weeks after they had killed her father.

About this time the disputes between the British government and the colonies began to run high, on account of the duties upon tea imported into this country; and much suspicion was entertained that the Indians were urged by the British agents to begin a war upon us, and to kill the traders then in the nation. However that might be, facts afterwards corroborated the suspicion.

The mouth of the Great Kenawha is distant from Camp Union about one hundred and sixty miles,—the way mountainous and rugged. At the time we commenced our march no track or path was made, and but few white men had ever seen the place. Our principal pilot was Captain Matthew Arbuckle. Our bread stuff was packed upon horses, and droves of cattle furnished our meat; of which we had a plentiful supply, as droves of cattle and pack-horses came in succession after us. But we went on expeditiously, under every disadvantage, and arrived at Point Pleasant about the 1st of October, where we expected the Earl of Dunmore would meet us with his army, who was to have come down the river from Fort Pitt, as was previously determined between the commanders. In this expectation we were greatly disappointed; for his lordship pursued a different route, and had taken his march from Pittsburg, by land, towards the Shawanee towns. General Lewis, finding himself disappointed in meeting the Governor and his army at Point Pleasant, despatched two scouts up the river, by land, to Fort Pitt, to endeavor to learn the cause of the disappointment; and our army remained encamped, to wait their return.

Before we marched from Camp Union, we were joined by Colonel John Fields, with a company of men from Culpeper, and Captain Thomas Buford, from Bedford county; also three other companies, under the command of Captain Evan Shelby, Captain William Russell, and Captain Harbert, from Holston, now Washington county. These troops were to compose a division commanded by Colonel William Christian, who was then convening more men in that quarter of the country, with a view of pursuing us to the mouth of the Great Kenawha, where the whole army were expected to meet, and proceed from thence to the Shawanee towns. The last mentioned companies completed our army to eleven hundred men.

During the time our scouts were going express up the river to Fort Pitt, the Governor had despatched three men, lately traders amongst the Indians, down the river, express to General Lewis, to inform him of his new plan and the route he was about to take, with instructions to pursue our march to the Shawanee towns, where he expected to assemble with us. But what calculations he might have made for delay or other disappointments which would be likely to happen to two armies under so long and difficult a march through a trackless wilderness, I never could guess; or how he could suppose they would assemble at a conjuncture so critical as the business then in question required, was never known to any body.

The Governor's express arrived at our encampment on Sunday, the 9th day of October,—and on that day it was my lot to command the guard. One of the men's name was M'Cullough, with whom I had made some acquaintance in Philadelphia, in the year 1766, at the Indian Queen, where we both happened to lodge. This man, supposing I was in Lewis's army, inquired and was told that I was on guard. He made it his business to visit me, to renew our acquaintance; and in the course of our conversation, he informed me he had recently left the Shawanee towns and gone to the Governor's camp. This made me desirous to know his opinion of our expected success in subduing the Indians, and whether he thought they would be presumptuous enough to offer to fight us, as we supposed we had a force superior to any thing they could oppose to us. He answered, "Aye, they will give you grinders, and that before long:" and repeating it with an oath, swore we would get grinders very soon. I believe that he and his companions left our camp that evening, to return to the Governor's camp. The next morning two young men had set out very early to hunt for deer; they happened to ramble up the (Ohio) river two or three miles, and on a sudden fell on the camp of the Indians, who had crossed the river the evening before, and were just about fixing for battle. They discovered the young men and fired upon them; one was killed, the other escaped, and got into our camp just before sunrise. He stopped just before my tent, and I discovered a number of men collecting round him as I lay in my bed. I jumped up and approached him to know what was the alarm, when I heard him declare that he had seen above five acres of land covered with Indians, as thick as they could stand one beside another.

General Lewis immediately ordered a detachment of Augusta troops, under his brother Colonel Charles Lewis, and another detachment of the Botetourt troops, under Colonel William Fleming. These were composed of the companies commanded by the oldest captains; and the junior captains were ordered to stay in camp, to aid the others as occasion would require. The detachments marched out in two lines, and met the Indians in the same order of march, about four hundred yards from our camp, and in sight of the guard. The Indians made the first fire and killed both the scouts in front of the two lines. Just as the sun was rising, a very heavy fire soon commenced, and Colonel Lewis was mortally wounded, but walked into camp and died a few minutes afterwards; observing to Colonel Charles Simms, with his last words, that he had sent one of the enemy to eternity before him. During his life it was his lot to have frequent skirmishes with the Indians, in which he was always successful; had gained much applause for his intrepidity, and was greatly beloved by his troops. Colonel Fleming was also wounded; and our men had given way some distance before they were reinforced by the other companies issuing in succession from the camp. The Indians in turn had to retreat, until they formed a line behind logs and trees, across from the bank of the Ohio to the bank of the Kenawha, and kept up their fire till sundown.

The Indians were exceedingly active in concealing their dead that were killed. I saw a young man draw out three, who were covered with leaves beside a large log, in the midst of the battle.

Colonel Christian came with troops to our camp that night, about eleven o'clock, General Lewis having despatched a messenger up the Kenawha to give him notice that we were engaged, and to hasten his march to our assistance. He brought about three hundred men with him, and marched out early next morning over the battle ground, and found twenty-one of the enemy slain on the ground.—

Twelve more were afterwards found, all concealed in one place; and the Indians confessed that they had thrown a number into the river in time of the battle; so that it is possible that the slain on both sides, were about equal. We had seventy-five killed, and one hundred and forty wounded. The Indians were headed by their chief, the Corn-stalk warrior; who, in his plan of attack and retreat, discovered great military skill. Amongst the slain on our side, were Colonel Charles Lewis, Colonel John Fields, Captain Buford, Captain Murray, Captain Ward, Captain Wilson, Captain Robert M'Clenachan, Lieutenant Allen, Lieutenant Goldsby, Lieutenant Dillon, and other subaltern officers. Colonel Fields had raised his company, I believe, under no particular instructions; and seemed, from the time he joined our army at Camp Union, to assume an independence, not subject to the control of others. His claim to such privileges might have arisen from some former military service in which he had been engaged, entitling him to a rank that ought to relieve him from being subject to control by volunteer commanders; and when we marched from Camp Union he took a separate route. On the third day after our departure, two of his men, of the name of Coward and Clay, who left the company to look after deer for provisions, as they marched fell in with two Indians, on the waters of the Little Meadows. As Clay passed round the root of a large log, under which one of the Indians was concealed, he killed Clay— and running up to scalp him, Coward killed him, being at some distance behind Clay. They both fell together, on the same spot. The other Indian fled, and passed our scouts unarmed. A bundle of ropes was found where they killed Clay, which proved that their intention was to steal horses. Colonel Fields joined us again that evening, and separated no more till we arrived at Point Pleasant, at the mouth of the Great Kenawha.

After the battle, we had different accounts of the number of Indians who attacked us. Some asserted that they were upwards of one thousand; some said no more than four or five hundred. The correct number was never known to us; however, it was certain they were combined of different nations—Shawanese, Wyandotts, and Delawares.—Of the former there is no doubt the whole strength of the nation was engaged in the battle. And on the evening of the day before the battle, when they were about to cross over the river, the Corn-stalk proposed to the Indians that if they were agreed, he would come and talk with us, and endeavor to make peace; but they would not listen to him. On the next day, as we were informed, he killed one of the Indians for retreating in the battle, in a cowardly manner. I could hear him the whole day speaking very loud to his men; and one of my company, who had once been a prisoner, told me what he was saying; encouraging the Indians,—telling them—"be strong, be strong!"

None will suppose that we had a contemptible enemy to do with, who has any knowledge of the exploits performed by them. It was chiefly the Shawanese that cut off the British army under General Braddock, in the year 1755, only nineteen years before our battle, where the General himself, and Sir Peter Hackett, second in command, were both slain, and a mere remnant of the whole army only escaped. It was they, too, who defeated Major Grant and his Scotch Highlanders, at Fort Pitt, in 1758, where the whole of the troops were killed and taken prisoners. After our battle, they defeated all the flower of the first bold and intrepid settlers of Kentucky, at the battle of the Blue Licks. There fell Colonel John Todd and Colonel Stephen Trigg. The whole of their men were almost cut to pieces. Afterwards they defeated the United States army, over the Ohio, commanded by General Harmar. And lastly, they defeated General Arthur St. Clair's great army, with prodigious slaughter. I believe it was never known that so many Indians were ever killed in any engagement with the white people, as fell by the army of General Lewis, at Point Pleasant. They are now dwindled to insignificance, and no longer noticed; and futurity will not easily perceive the prowess they possessed.

Of all the Indians, the Shawanese were the most bloody and terrible,—holding all other men, as well Indians as whites, in contempt as warriors, in comparison with themselves. This opinion made them more wrestless and fierce than any other savages; and they boasted that they had killed ten times as many white people as any other Indians did. They were a well-formed, active, and ingenious people—were assuming and imperious in the presence of others not of their own nation, and sometimes very cruel.

General Lewis's army consisted chiefly of young volunteers, well trained to the use of arms, as hunting, in those days, was much practised, and preferred to agricultural pursuits by enterprising young men. The produce of the soil was of little value on the west side of the Blue Ridge—the ways bad, and the distance to market too great to make it esteemed. Such pursuits inured them to hardships and danger. We had more than every fifth man in our army killed or wounded in the battle,—but none were disheartened; all crossed the river with cheerfulness, bent on destroying the enemy; and had they not been restrained by the Governor's orders, I believe they would have exterminated the Shawanese nation.

This battle was, in fact, the beginning of the revolutionary war that obtained for our country the liberty and independence enjoyed by the United States, (and a good presage of future success;) for it is well known that the Indians were influenced by the British to commence the war to terrify and confound the people, before they commenced hostilities themselves the following year at Lexington, in Massachusetts. It was thought by British politicians, that to excite an Indian war would prevent a combination of the colonies for opposing Parliamentary measures to tax the Americans. The blood, therefore, spilt upon this memorable battle, will long be remembered by the good people of Virginia and the United States with gratitude.

The Indians passed over the Ohio river in the night time, after the battle, and made the best of their way back to the Shawanee towns, upon the Scioto. And, after burying our dead, General Lewis or-

7

dered entrenchments to be made around our camp, extending across from the Ohio to the Kenawha, to secure the officer, with an adequate number of men, to protect them in safety, and marched the army across the Ohio for the Shawanee towns.

In this command he had many difficulties to encounter, that none can well judge of who have never experienced similar troubles, to preserve order and necessary discipline, over an army of volunteers who had no knowledge of the use of discipline or military order, when in an enemy's country, well skilled in their own manner of warfare. And let it be remembered that the youth of our country, previous to those times, had grown up in times of peace, and were quite unacquainted with military operations of any kind. Ignorance of these duties, together with high notions of independence and equality of condition, rendered the service extremely difficult and disagreeable to the commander,—who was, by nature, of a lofty and high military spirit, and who had seen much military service under General Braddock and other commanders. He was appointed First Captain under General Washington, together with Captain Peter Hogg, in the year 1752, when General Washington was appointed Major by Governor Gooch, to go to the frontiers and erect a garrison at the Little Meadows, on the waters of the Monongahela, to prevent the encroachments of the French, who were extending their claims from Port Pitt (then Fort De Quesne) up the Monongahela river and its waters. During the time they were employed about that business, they sustained an attack, made on them by a party of French and Indians, sent out from Fort De Quesne for that purpose, on account of an unfortunate affair that took place soon after they had arrived at the Little Meadows. A French gentleman of the name of Jumenvail, with a party, was making some surveys not far from Major Washington's encampment, who ordered Captain Hogg to go and examine him as to his authority for making such encroachments on the British claims and settlements. Captain Hogg discovered Jumenvail's encampment, which he approached in the night time; and, contrary to his orders, or the instructions of Major Washington, he fired on Jumenvail and killed him. The French, in order to retaliate, sent out a party to attack Washington. They were discovered when within one mile of the encampment, and soon appeared before it, commencing firing as they approached. Our people had made some entrenchments, from which they returned the fire. In this engagement General Lewis received two wounds. The French at length cried out for a parly; the firing ceased on both sides; the parties intermixed indiscriminately, and articles of capitulation were drawn up by the French, which Major Washington signed and acknowledged. He was then a very young man, and unacquainted with the French language; and, it seems, that in that instrument he acknowledged the assassination of Jumenvail. This was sent to Europe, and published. Hostilities soon after commenced between the two rival nations, England and France, the chief foundation of the quarrel being this transaction in America. I have seen Bliss's account of the beginning of the war of 1755, in his history of England. It differs somewhat from this; but I have narrated the facts as I heard them from General Lewis, and have no doubt of their being correct.

The French had brought in their party a large number of Indians, which gave them a great superiority of numbers. An accident took place during the intermixture of the parties, which might have proved fatal to Washington and his party, had not General Lewis, with great presence of mind, prevented it. An Irish soldier in the crowd seeing an Indian near him, swore, in the well known language of his country, that he would " send the yellow son-of-a-bitch to hell." General Lewis was limping near him with his wounded leg, struck the muzzle of his gun into the air and saved the Indian's life, and the lives of all the party, had the Irishman's intention taken effect.

When the war of 1755 began, General Washington was appointed the commander of the first regiment ever raised in Virginia, and General Lewis, Major. Lewis was afterwards on a command with the British Major Grant, under General Forbis, to reconnoitre the vicinity of the French fort, (now Fort Pitt) against which General Forbis's army was then on their march, to endeavor to demolish.— When Grant and Lewis drew near the garrison undiscovered, Major Grant began to apprehend that he could surprise the garrison, and disappoint his General of the honor of the conquest. Against this unjustifiable attempt, General Lewis in vain remonstrated. He represented that the garrison was reinforced by a number of Indians, then at the place in great force, and the difficulty of reaching the garrison privately and undiscovered. Grant, however, was unwilling to share so great an honor with any other, and ordered Major Lewis to remain with their baggage, with the provincial troops which he commanded,—whilst he, with his Scotch Highlanders, advanced to the attack; which he began early in the morning, by beating drums upon Grant's hill, as it is still called. The Indians were lying on the opposite side of the river from the garrison, when the alarm began, in number about one thousand five hundred. The sound of war, so sudden and so near them, soon roused them to arms; and Grant and his Highlanders were soon surrounded, when the work of death went on rapidly, and in a manner quite novel to Scotch Highlanders, who, in all their European wars, had never before seen men's heads skinned. General Lewis soon perceived, by the retreating fire, that Major Grant was overmatched and in a bad situation. He advanced with his two hundred provincials, and falling on the rear of the Indians, made way for Major Grant and some of his men to escape; but Lewis's party was also defeated, and himself taken prisoner. The Indians desired to put him to death, but the French, with difficulty, saved him; however, the Indians stripped him of all his clothes, save his shirt, before he was taken into the fort. An elderly Indian seized the shirt, and insisted upon having it; but he resisted, with the tomahawk drawn over his head, until a French officer, by signs, requested him to deliver the shirt, and then took him into his room and gave him a complete dress to put on. When he was advancing to the relief of Grant, he met a Scotch Highlander under speedy flight; and inquiring of him how the battle was going, he said they were "a beaten, and he had seen Donald M'Donald up to his hunkers in mud, and a the skeen af his heed." Grant had made his escape from the field of battle with a party of seven or eight soldiers, and wandered all night in the woods. In the morning they returned to the garrison and surrendered themselves to the Indians, who carried them into the fort. Major Grant's life was preserved by the French; but the Indians brought the soldiers to the room door where Major Lewis was, where his benefactor refused to let them come in, and they killed all the men at the door.

The French, expecting that the main army, under General Forbis, would soon come on, and believing that they would not be able to defend the attack, blew up the fort and retreated to Quebec, with the prisoners, where they were confined till a cartel took place, and they were exchanged.

This is the same Colonel Grant who figured in the British Parliament in the year 1775, when Mr. Thurlow, the Attorney General, affirmed that the Americans were rebels and traitors,—but did not prove his position by comparison of their conduct with the treason laws; and Colonel Grant in particular, told the house that he had often acted in the same service with the Americans; he knew them well; and from that knowledge, would venture to predict— "that they would never dare to face an English army, as being destitute of every requisite to constitute good soldiers. By their laziness, uncleanliness, or radical defects of constitution, they were incapable of going through the service of a campaign, and would melt away with sickness before they would face an enemy, so that a very slight force would be more than sufficient for their complete reduction."* But during the time of their captivity, this philosophical hero was detected in an act of the most base hypocrisy, in Quebec. As the

* See History of England for 1775, vol. xii. p. 527,

letters of the English officers were not suffered to be sealed until they were inspected before they were sent off, a French officer discovered in Major Grant's communication to General Forbis, that he had ascribed the whole disgrace of his defeat to the misconduct of Major Lewis and his provincial troops. The officer immediately carried the letter to Major Lewis, and showed it to him. Lewis, indignant at such a scandalous and unjust representation, accused Grant of his duplicity, in the presence of the French officers, and challenged him; but Grant prudently declined the combat, after receiving the grossest insults, by spitting in his face, and degrading language.

After the French had blown up the fort and departed for Quebec with the prisoners, in going up the Alleghany river it was very cold, and Grant lay shivering in the boat, cursing the Americans and their country,—threatening that if he ever returned to England he would let his majesty know their insignificance, and the impropriety of the trouble and expense to the nation in endeavoring to protect such a vile country and people. For this provoking language, General Lewis did chide him severely.

General Lewis was, in person, upwards of six feet high, of uncommon strength and agility, and his form of the most exact symmetry that I ever beheld in human being. He had a stern and invincible countenance, and was of a reserved and distant deportment, which rendered his presence more awful than engaging. He was a commissioner, with Dr. Thomas Walker, to hold a treaty, on behalf of the colony of Virginia, with the six nations of Indians, together with the commissioners from Pennsylvania, New York, and other eastern provinces, held at Fort Stanevix, in the province of New York, in the year 1768. It was there remarked by the Governor of New York, that "the earth seemed to tremble under him as he walked along." His independent spirit despised sycophantic means of gaining popularity, which never rendered more than his merits extorted.

Such a character was not calculated to gain much applause by commanding an army of volunteers without discipline, experience, or gratitude. Many took umbrage because they were compelled to do their duty; others thought the duties of a common soldier were beneath the dignity of a volunteer. Every one found some cause of imaginary complaint.

When congress determined to be independent, and appointed general officers to command our armies to prosecute the war for independence and defending our liberty, they nominated General Washington to the chief command,—who, from his great modesty, recommended General Lewis in preference to himself; but one of his colleagues from Virginia, observed that General Lewis's popularity had suffered much from the declamation of some of his troops, on the late expedition against the Indians, and that it would be impolitic at that conjuncture, to make the appointment. He was, however, afterwards appointed among the first brigadier generals, and took the command, at Norfolk, of the Virginia troops. When Lord Dunmore made his escape from Williamsburg, on board a British ship of war lying off Norfolk, the vessel drew up and commenced a fire on the town; but General Lewis, from a battery, compelled his lordship to depart,—and, I believe, he never afterwards set foot on American ground. This ended the military career of General Lewis. Congress having appointed General Stevens and some other major generals, gave him some offence. He had been their superior in former services. Having accepted his office of brigadier at the solicitation of General Washington, he wrote to the General of his intention to resign. General Washington, in reply, pressed him to hold his command, and assured him that justice would be done him as respected his rank. But he was grown old, his ardor for military fame abated; and being seized with a fever resigned his command to return home, in the year 1780. He died on his way, in Bedford county, about forty miles from his own house, on Roanoke, in Botetourt county, lamented by all who were intimately acquainted with his meritorious services and superior qualities.

It is said that there is a book now extant, in this country, with the title of "Smith's Travels in America," which was written in England, wherein the author asserts that he was on the expedition in the year 1774, and that he joined the Augusta troops in Staunton. He gives a particular description of Mr. Sampson Matthew's tavern and family, who kept the most noted public house in town, and of the march of our army from Camp Union to Point Pleasant. He also gives an account of the battle, and of Colonel Lewis being killed in the engagement. If such a person was along, I am persuaded he was *in cog*, and a creature of Lord Dunmore; for I was particularly acquainted with all the officers of the Augusta troops, and the chief of all the men, but knew no such man as Smith. I am the more confirmed in this opinion from what General Lewis told me in the year 1779, that he was well informed that on the evening of the 10th October, the day of our battle, Dunmore and the noted Doctor Connelly, of tory memory, with some other officers, were taking a walk, when Dunmore observed to the gentlemen that he expected by that time Colonel Lewis had hot work. This corresponds with my suspicions of the language of M'Cullough, who promised us "grinders." Had not M'Cullough seen the Indians, coming down the river and on his return, the evening before the battle, they could not have known the strength of our army, or amount of our troops so correctly as they certainly did; for, during the battle, I heard one of the enemy halloo, with abusive terms in English, that they had eleven hundred Indians, and two thousand coming. The same boast was vociferated from the opposite side of the river, in the hearing of most of our officers and men who occupied the Ohio bank, during the battle. As the number mentioned, of eleven hundred, was precisely our number, and the expectation entertained by some, that Colonel Christian would come on with two thousand more, the intelligence must have been communicated to the Indians by the Governor's scouts, for there could have been no other means of conveying such exact information to them. Colonel Christian had but three hundred altogether, including the companies of Shelby, Russell, and Harbert, when he arrived at our camp.

Having finished the entrenchments, and put every thing in order for securing the wounded from danger after the battle, we crossed the Ohio river in our march to the Shawanee towns. Captain Arbuckle was our guide, who was equally esteemed as a soldier and a fine woodsman. When we came to the prairie, on Killicanic creek, we saw the smoke of a small Indian town, which was deserted and set on fire upon our approach. Here we met an express from the Governor's camp, who had arrived near the nation and proposed peace to the Indians. Some of the chiefs, with the Grenadier Squaw, on the return of the Indians after their defeat, had repaired to the Governor's army to solicit terms of peace for the Indians, which I apprehend they had no doubt of obtaining. The Governor promised them the war should be no further prosecuted, and that he would stop the march of Lewis's army before any more hostilities should be committed upon them. However, the Indians finding we were rapidly approaching, began to suspect that the Governor did not possess the power of stopping us, whom they designated by the name of the Big Knife Men; the Governor, therefore, with the White Fish warrior, set off and met us at Killicanic creek, and there Colonel Lewis received his orders-to return with his army, as he had proposed terms of peace with the Indians, which he assured should be accomplished.

His lordship requested Colonel Lewis to introduce him to his officers; and we were accordingly ranged in rank, and had the honor of an introduction to the Governor and commander in chief, who politely thanked us for services rendered on so momentous an occasion, and assured us of his high esteem and respect for our conduct.

On the Governor's consulting Colonel Lewis, it was deemed necessary that a garrison should be established at Point Pleasant, to intercept and prevent the Indians from crossing the Ohio to our side, as also to prevent any whites from crossing over to the side of the

8

Indians; and by such means to preserve a future peace, according to the conditions of the treaty then to be made by the Governor with the Indians. Captain Arbuckle was appointed commander of the garrison, with instructions to enlist one hundred men, for the term of one year from the date of their enlistment, and proceed to erect a fort, which was executed in the following summer.

The next spring, the revolutionary war commenced between the British army, under General Gage, at Boston, and the citizens of the state of Massachusetts, at Lexington. Virginia soon after assumed an independent form of government, and began to levy troops for the common defence, when another company was ordered to the aid of Captain Arbuckle, to be commanded by Captain William M'Kee. But the troubles of the war accumulated so fast, that it was it was found too inconvenient and expensive to keep a garrison, at so great an expense and so great a distance from any inhabitants. There was, also, a demand for all the troops that could be raised, to oppose British force, and Captain Arbuckle was ordered to vacate the station and to join General Washington's army. This he was not willing to do, having engaged, as he alleged, for a different service. A number of his men, however, marched and joined the main army until the time of their enlistment expired.

In the year 1777, the Indians, being urged by British agents, became very troublesome to frontier settlements, manifesting much appearance of hostilities, when the Corn-stalk warrior, with the Red-hawk, paid a visit to the garrison at Point Pleasant. He made no secret of the disposition of the Indians; declaring that, on his own part, he was opposed to joining in the war on the side of the British, but that all the nation, except himself and his own tribe, were determined to engage in it; and that, of course, he and his tribe would have to run with the stream, (as he expressed it.) On this Captain Arbuckle thought proper to detain him, the Red-hawk, and another fellow, as hostages, to prevent the nation from joining the British.

In the course of that summer our government had ordered an army to be raised, of volunteers, to serve under the command of General Hand; who was to have collected a number of troops at Fort Pitt, with them to descend the river to Point Pleasant, there to meet a reinforcement of volunteers expected to be raised in Augusta and Botetourt counties, and then proceed to the Shawanee towns and chastize them so as to compel them to a neutrality. Hand did not succeed in the collection of troops at Fort Pitt; and but three or four companies were raised in Augusta and Botetourt, which were under the command of Colonel George Skillern, who ordered me to use my endeavors to raise all the volunteers I could get in Greenbrier, for that service. The people had begun to see the difficulties attendant on a state of war and long campaigns carried through wildernesses, and but a few were willing to engage in such service. But as the settlements which we covered, though less exposed to the depredations of the Indians, had showed their willingness to aid in the proposed plan to chastize the Indians, and had raised three companies, I was very desirous of doing all I could to promote the business and aid the service. I used the utmost endeavors, and proposed to the militia officers to volunteer ourselves, which would be an encouragement to others, and by such means to raise all the men who could be got. The chief of the officers in Greenbrier agreed to the proposal, and we cast lots who should command the company. The lot fell on Andrew Hamilton for captain, and William Renick lieutenant. We collected in all, about forty, and joined Colonel Skillern's party, on their way to Point Pleasant.

When we arrived, there was no account of General Hand or his army, and little or no provision made to support our troops, other than what we had taken with us down the Kenawha. We found, too, that the garrison was unable to spare us any supplies, having nearly exhausted, when we got there, what had been provided for themselves. But we concluded to wait there as long as we could for the arrival of General Hand, or some account from him. During the time of our stay two young men, of the names of Hamilton and

Gilmore, went over the Kenawha one day to hunt for deer; on their return to camp, some Indians had concealed themselves on the bank amongst the weeds, to view our encampment; and as Gilmore came along past them, they fired on him and killed him on the bank.

Captain Arbuckle and myself were standing on the opposite bank when the gun fired; and whilst we were wondering who it could be shooting, contrary to orders, or what they were doing over the river, we saw Hamilton run down the bank, who called out that Gilmore was killed. Gilmore was one of the company of Captain John Hall, of that part of the country now Rockbridge county. The captain was a relation of Gilmore's, whose family and friends were chiefly cut off by the Indians, in the year 1763, when Greenbrier was cut off. Hall's men instantly jumped into a canoe and went to the relief of Hamilton, who was standing in momentary expectation of being put to death. They brought the corpse of Gilmore down the bank, covered with blood and scalped, and put him into the canoe. As they were passing the river, I observed to Captain Arbuckle that the people would be for killing the hostages, as soon as the canoe would land. He supposed that they would not offer to commit so great a violence upon the innocent, who were in nowise accessary to the murder of Gilmore. But the canoe had scarcely touched the shore until the cry was raised, let us kill the Indians in the fort;— and every man, with his gun in his hand, came up the bank pale with rage. Captain Hall was at their head, and leader. Captain Arbuckle and I met them, and endeavored to dissuade them from so unjustifiable an action; but they cocked their guns, threatened us with instant death if we did not desist, rushed by us into the fort, and put the Indians to death.

On the preceding day, the Corn-stalk's son, Elinipsico, had come from the nation to see his father, and to know if he was well, or alive. When he came to the river opposite the fort, he hallooed. His father was, at that instant, in the act of delineating a map of the country and the waters between the Shawanee towns and the

Mississippi, at our request, with chalk upon the floor. He immediately recognized the voice of his son, got up, went out, and answered him. The young fellow crossed over, and they embraced each other in the most tender and affectionate manner. The interpreter's wife, who had been a prisoner among the Indians, and had recently left them on hearing the uproar the next day; and hearing the men threatening that they would kill the Indians, for whom she retained much affection, ran to their cabin and informed them that the people were just coming to kill them; and that, because the Indians who killed Gilmore, had come with Elinipsico the day before. He utterly denied it; declared that he knew nothing of them, and trembled exceedingly. His father encouraged him not to be afraid, for that the Great Man above had sent him there to be killed and die with him. As the men advanced to the door, the Corn-stalk rose up and met them; they fired upon him, and seven or eight bullets went through him. So fell the great Corn-stalk warrior,—whose name was bestowed upon him by the consent of the nation, as their great strength and support. His son was shot dead, as he sat upon a stool. The Red-hawk made an attempt to go up the chimney, but was shot down. The other Indian was shamefully mangled, and I grieved to see him so long in the agonies of death.

The Corn-stalk, from personal appearance and many brave acts, was undoubtedly a hero. Had he been spared to live, I believe he would have been friendly to the American cause; for nothing could induce him to make the visit to the garrison at the critical time he did, but to communicate to them the temper and disposition of the Indians, and their design of taking part with the British. On the day he was killed we held a council, at which he was present. His countenance was dejected; and he made a speech, all of which seemed to indicate an honest and manly disposition. He acknowledged that he expected that he and his party would have to run with the stream, for that all the Indians on the lakes and northwardly, were joining the British. He said that when he returned to the Shawanee towns after the battle at the Point, he called a council of the nation to consult what was to be done, and upbraided them for their folly in not suffering him to make peace on the evening before the battle.—" What," said he, " will you do now? The Big Knife is coming on us, and we shall all be killed. Now you must fight, or we are undone." But no one made an answer. He said, then let us kill all our women and children, and go and fight till we die. But none would answer. At length he rose and struck his tomahawk in the post in the centre of the town house: " I'll go," said he, " and make peace ;" and then the warriors all grunted out " ough, ough, ough," and runners were instantly despatched to the Governor's army to solicit a peace and the interposition of the Governor on their behalf.

When he made his speech in council with us, he seemed to be impressed with an awful premonition of his approaching fate ; for he repeatedly said, " When I was a young man and went to war, I thought that might be the last time, and I would return no more. Now I am here amongst you ; you may kill me if you please ; I can die but once ; and it is all one to me, now or another time." This declaration concluded every sentence of his speech. He was killed about one hour after our council.

A few days after this catastrophe General Hand arrived, but had no troops. We were discharged, and returned home a short time before Christmas. Not long after we left the garrison a small party of Indians appeared hear the fort, and Lieutenant Moore was ordered, with a party, to pursue them. Their design was to retaliate the murder of Corn-stalk. Moore had not pursued one-quarter of a mile until he fell into an ambuscade and was killed, with several of his men.

The next year, 1778, in the month of May, a small party of Indians again appeared near the garrison, and showed themselves and decamped apparently in great terror. But the garrison was aware of their seduction, and no one was ordered to pursue them. Finding that their scheme was not likely to succeed, their whole army rose up at once and showed themselves, extending across from the bank of the Ohio to the bank of the Kenawha, and commenced firing upon the garrison, but without effect, for several hours. At length one of them had the presumption to advance so near the fort as to request the favor of being permitted to come in, to which Captain M'Kee granted his assent, and the stranger very composedly walked in. Captain Arbuckle was then absent, on a visit in Greenbrier, to his family. During the time the strange gentleman was in the fort, a gun went off in the fort, by accident. The Indians without, raised a hideous yell, supposing the fellow was killed; but he instantly jumped up into one of the bastions and showed himself, giving the sign that all was well, and reconciled his friends. Finding that they could make no impression upon the garrison, they concluded to come on to Greenbrier; and collecting all the cattle about the garrison, for provision on their march, set off up the Kenawha, in great military parade, to finish their campaign and take vengeance on us for the death of Corn-stalk. Captain M'Kee perceiving their design, by the route they were pursuing, despatched Philip Hammond and John Prior after them, with orders, if possible to pass them undiscovered, and to give the inhabitants notice of their approach. This hazardous service they performed with great fidelity. The Indians had two days start of them, but they pursued with such speed and diligence, that they overtook and passed the Indians at the house of William M'Clung, at the Meadows, about twenty miles from Lewisburg. It was in the evening of the day, and M'Clung's family had previously removed farther in amongst the inhabitants for safety, as they were the frontier family on the way to Point Pleasant. At this place Hammond and Prior had a full view of the Indians, as they walked upon a rising ground between the house and the barn, and appeared to be viewing the great meadows lying in sight of the house. Hammond and Prior were in the meadows, concealed by the weeds, and had a full view of their whole party undiscovered, and calculated their numbers at about two hundred warriors. Having passed the Indians, they came on in great speed, to Colonel Donnally's, and gave the alarm of the approach of the Indians. Colonel Donnally lost no time to collect in all his nearest neighbors that night, and sent a servant to my house to inform me. Before day about twenty men, including Hammond and Prior, were collected at Donnally's, and they had the advantage of a stockade fort around and adjoining the house. There was a number of women and children, making in all about sixty persons in the house. On the next day they kept a good look-out, in momentary expectation of the enemy.

Colonel Samuel Lewis was at my house when Donnally's servant came with the intelligence; and we lost no time in alarming the people, and to collect as many men for defence, as we could get at Camp Union all the next day. But all were busy; some flying with their families to the inward settlements, and others securing their property,—so that in the course of the day, we had not collected near one hundred men. On the following day we sent out two scouts to Donnally's, very early in the morning, who soon returned with intelligence that the fort was attacked. The scouts had got within one mile, and heard the guns firing briskly. We determined to give all the aid we could to the besieged, and every man who was willing to go was paraded. They amounted to sixty-eight in all, including Colonel Lewis, Captain Arbuckle, and myself. We drew near Donnally's house about two o'clock P. M. but heard no firing. For the sake of expedition we had left the road for a nearer way, which led to the back side of the house, and thus escaped falling into an ambuscade, placed on the road some distance from the house, which might hnve been fatal to us, being greatly inferior to the enemy in numbers. We soon discovered Indians, behind trees in a rye-field, looking earnestly at the house. Charles Gatliff and I fired upon them, when we saw others running in the rye, near where they stood. We all ran directly to the fort. The people, on hearing the guns on the back side of the house, supposed that it was another party of Indians, and all were at the port holes ready to fire upon us;

but some discovering that we were their friends, opened the gate, and we all got in safe. One man only, was shot through his clothes.

When we got into the fort, we found that there were only four men killed. Two of them who were coming to the fort, fell into the midst of the Indians, and were killed. A servant of Donnally's was killed early in the morning on the first attack; and one man was killed in a bastion in the fort. The Indians had commenced their attack about daylight in the morning, when the people were all in bed, except Philip Hammond and an old negro. The house formed one part of the fort, and was double, the kitchen making one end of the house, and there Hammond and the negro were. A hogshead of water was placed against the door. The enemy had laid down their guns at a stable, about fifty yards from the house, and made their attacks with tomahawks and war clubs. Hammond and the negro held the door till they were splitting it with their tomahawks: they suddenly let the door open, and Hammond killed the Indian on the threshold, who was splitting the door. The negro had a musket charged with swan shot, and was jumping about in the floor asking Hammond where he should shoot? Hammond bade him fire away amongst them; for the yard was crowded as thick as they could stand. Dick fired away, and I believe, with good effect; for a war club lay in the yard with a swan shot in it. Dick is now upwards of eighty years old, has long been abandoned by his master, as also his wife, as aged as himself, and they have made out to support their miserable existence, many years past, by their own endeavors. This is the negro to whom our assembly, at its last session, refused to grant a small pension to support the short remainder of his wretched days, which must soon end, although his humble petition was supported by certificates of the most respectable men in the county, of his meritorious service on this occasion, which saved the lives of many citizens then in the house.

The firing of Hammond and Dick awakened the people in the other end of the house, and up stairs, where the chief of the men

9

were lying. They soon fired out of the windows on the Indians so briskly, that when we got to the fort, seventeen of them lay dead in the yard, one of whom was a boy about fifteen or sixteen years old—his body was so torn by the bullets that a man might have run his arm through him, yet he lived almost all day, and made a most lamentable cry. The Indians called to him to go into the house.

After dark, a fellow drew near to the fort and called out in english that he wanted to make peace. We invited him in to consult on the terms, but he declined our civility. They departed that night, after dragging eight of their slain out of the yard; but we never afterwards found where they buried them. They visited Greenbrier but twice afterwards, and then in very small parties, one of which killed a man and his wife, of the name of Munday, and wounded Capt. Samuel McClung. The last person killed was Thomas Griffith,—his son was taken, but going down the Kenawha, they were pursued, one of the Indians was killed, and the boy was relieved, which ended our wars in Greenbrier with the Indians, in the year 1780.

[Signed,]　　JOHN STUART.

The above is a correct copy from the original, in my possession, with slight variations of orthography and punctuation. I do not know at what date it was written.

CH: A. STUART.

January 14th, 1833.

[☞Although the following letter from CHARLES A. STUART, Esq. respecting the preceding narrative—was not designed for publication, the standing committee, have considered it expedient to insert it,—and for so doing trust to the writer's indulgence.]

JANUARY 15th, 1833.

Dear Sir,

I, yesterday, sent to your brother to be forwarded, the copy of my father's narrative, which I, some time ago, promised to supply, at your request for Gen. Brodnax. There may be, and I think probably are, some historical inaccuracies in it, in respect to transactions, at a distance from the scene of his own experience and observation. I say "probably are," because there are some slight discrepancies between his statements and those of Gen. Marshall's history, touching the same incidents. The latter is doubtless, founded upon Gen. Washington's relation of the facts, who, from his situation, may readily be supposed to be more accurately informed than Gen. Lewis was. But, be this as it may, my father's narrative of such details is, unquestionably, as he received them from Gen. Lewis; and as little question can there be, that the latter related them precisely as he apprehended them.

As to the facts stated as within the observation of the narrator himself, his station, his character, and the traditions still current throughout the region of their occurrence, abundantly sustain them. Indeed, the modesty with which the narrative proceeds, pretermitting numerous amusing anecdotes which he used to relate to his acquaintances and with which I have often known him and his old associates to recreate themselves, is strong internal evidence, at least to me, of the scrupulous care with which he has related this history of his experience.

It will be obvious, from the texture of the narrative, that he was uneducated and unaccustomed to indite history.

Lapse of time, and lapse of life are fast extinguishing the traditions

> —— "Of most disastrous chances,
> "Of moving accidents, by flood and field;
> "Of hair-breadth scapes,"—

and all the hazards of border life and frontier adventure. Yet many of those traditions might yet be rescued from total extinguishment. There are still living a number of old (they are now very old) persons who would love to

> ——"Speak of some distressful stroke
> That (their) youth suffered."—

I cannot now recall many to my remembrance; but I recollect Mr. Wm. Arbuckle on Kenawha, who I believe is still living, and Mrs. Erskine of Monroe, who saw and heard much, and like all others, in the advance of years, would doubtless, dilate with pleasure, upon the reminiscences of youth.

Your friend,

CH. A. STUART.

To THOMAS JEFFERSON STUART, Esq
Richmond, Virginia.